Belonging to Borders

Belonging to Borders
A Sojourn in the Celtic Tradition

Bonnie Bowman Thurston

Foreword by
Esther de Waal

LITURGICAL PRESS
Collegeville, Minnesota

www.litpress.org

1   2   3   4   5   6   7   8   9

Library of Congress Cataloging-in-Publication Data

Thurston, Bonnie Bowman.
    Belonging to borders : a sojourn in the Celtic tradition /
  Bonnie Bowman Thurston.
       p. cm.
    Includes bibliographical references.
    ISBN 978-0-8146-3367-0
    1. Spirituality—Celtic Church.   2. Spirituality—Ireland.
  3. Spirituality—Wales.   4. Spirituality—Scotland.   I. Title.
  BR743.3.T48 2011
  270.2089'916—dc22   2010053965

Peregrinatio pro eterna patria

+++

You are fire as a poem is,
element of the phoenix.

— *"Hymn to St. Ffraid,"* Ruth Bidgood[1]

1. Ruth Bidgood, *Symbols of Plenty* (Norwich: Canterbury Press, 2006), 12.

Contents

Foreword

There is a question that is asked in Wales: Where do you come from? Where are you in your roots? That is a question that all of us must ask, both literally and metaphorically, if we are to live fully and freely. Here, in answering that for herself, Bonnie Thurston draws us, her readers, into that quest. As she discovers her role as a person of the borders, and draws strength and inspiration from the ancient Celtic tradition of those areas of Britain where that flourished in the early centuries, she makes it a journey in which we can all share.

The Celtic lands of Ireland, Scotland, and Wales which figure in this book are places where words become song, where words take flight, and not least those words which deal with what is innermost in our hearts. Theology in the Celtic tradition was never the preserve of professional theologians, and there is a delightful myth that a professor of theology at one of the leading Welsh universities today will tell his students that if they have come in search of theology they should "ask the poets." This making of theological truth into song and verse in the Christian era followed on as a natural continuation from the role of the bards employed in the courts of warrior kings to sing their praises. These new bards now sang the praises of a King who was both creator and redeemer rescuing them from the powers of darkness, inner and outer, and bringing them into a new freedom—which yet did not reject but which built on what had gone before.

One of the peculiar strengths of the Celtic tradition is its sense of the elemental, its connectedness with earth and stone, with fire and water, with clouds and rain. All these run as threads through the following pages and time and time again arrest us with the simplicity and power with which Bonnie uses her words to capture them. In these poems she is quietly reminding us to remain earthed and grounded in *this* reality. She is giving us the defense that contemporary society needs against the virtual reality that everywhere seems to be creeping up on us, besieging us with its all-too-easy accessibility. Instead, this book will remind us of "rock that gives substance, solidity, / a place for permanent belonging" (p. 43). Above all here we will be helped to recover elemental beauty (p. 48).

The "stark solidity of elemental things" (p. 46) is a most attractive phrase, coming significantly in a poem titled "The Christ of Iona." You cannot read this book without being reminded of the important role of the tactile inherent in wood and rock, to feel the sense of touching stone. She allows us to stand there alongside her as she dares to place her hand on those megaliths, great stones in a field where, as she touches their rough-hewn sides, she feels "a faint, throbbing beat" (p. 90), aware of the energy that resonates around them.

This sense of the closeness of the natural elements and of their powers, is, as the poems show time and again, something found in the lives of the great Celtic saints. When St. David preaches, "the earth itself / rose up beneath his feet" (p. 10) St. Columba sometimes sees the heavens on fire, sometimes feels one with the winds "of this pulsating place" (p. 14). But it is also there for us to rediscover, and the simplicity of her words allow the elements themselves to speak: "The howl of wind, dark sky, / rain blown horizontally" (p. 79). The power of the earth, the elements, the four seasons, equinox and solstice, woven together, are experienced by her in Iona, whose opening lines lay this bare: "Iona's holiness and healing / is in the confluence of elemental things, / the wind that gathers primeval waters" (p. 43).

If we are to touch, to rediscover, what is primeval in the external world, what about the primal within ourselves? The breaking down of barriers, the bringing together of differing elements into a creative whole, is surely the gift that the experience of the borders brings to those who seek out their ancient wisdom. Above all it is in the wholeness that comes from the acceptance of the pre-Christian and its giftedness being incorporated into Christian understanding that comes over so forcefully in her poem "Green Man" (p. 64). Lurking around in the corner of a small church, such as at Rowlestone, gazing down imperiously from the central boss in the vaulted roof of the nave of a Cistercian abbey at Dore, it speaks of something never written down in those early days but that now can be best captured in poetic words. As we read her poem, Bonnie confronts us with the presence of a whole world of inner, secret knowledge of the livingness of matter, the whole natural world as a living thing, of which we, as humans, are a part. Are her final words a triumphant shout, a quiet prayer? Both of course: "Root it deep within us, / this healing wholeness, / this wild profusion of life" (p. 65).

It is no wonder that the Welsh Borders should have drawn her, and that coming here she should immediately have felt herself drawn into kinship with the place and its people. Kinship is a form of relationship that underlies many other relationships, the connectedness of sharing common interests and concerns, whether human or nonhuman. So here Bonnie was welcomed and came to know what is given to us who have the great good fortune to be rooted here: holy places, legends and myths, time-less mysteries of ancient trackways, Celtic wells and shrines, mountains and small streams—that ever-changing landscape, with its pattern of hill rhythms and water rhythms. David Jones, artist and poet, who drew inspiration from the years that he spent in the Black Mountains, found that there was no stillness in this landscape but that the movement of streams, wind, rain, and cloud ceaselessly transform—in change which reveals the unchanging.

A borders person herself, in her family and in her geog-raphy, Bonnie Thurston delights in finding across the Atlantic places that connect her with her deepest understanding and instincts. Since Thomas Merton has been a profound inspira-tion in her life, and she has applied her very fine scholarship to deepening our knowledge of this complex and kaleidoscopic man, we can appreciate how his understanding of the role of "one good place" can be held in tension with the movement of spirit, the interior journey of self-discovery and growth into the knowledge of God.

All these differing elements flow into a book that is made for gentle, slow, prayerful reading—a book to return to time and again, at different times and seasons of the year, of our life. She takes us behind the all-too-easy trivializing of the Celtic which in recent years has popularized something that should remain mysterious, elusive, something to be handled with reverence and respect.

Esther de Waal
The Feast of St. Michael and All Angels

The Autobiographical Why

This is an odd little book, part church history, part spirituality, mostly poetry. It opens with a bit of autobiography because its hybrid nature may make more sense if you know something about its author. I was born deep in the southern mountains of West Virginia, born to that landscape from progenitors with the great family names of Britain, Wales, Scotland: Bowman, Morris, King, Lewis, Wells, names occurring in those islands long before the Norman invasion. These people were storytellers and singers. I heard poetry for as long as I can remember. My father quoted it. My brother maintains Dad had to memorize poetry as punishment for being naughty in school, and, truth be told, my Dad's nickname in his family was "Naughty." When somebody called on the phone and asked for "Naught," we knew it was paternal kinfolk. And I heard song. My mother, who by her own admission "couldn't carry a tune in a bucket," sang to me. Hymns. When I hear, as I still occasionally do in church, "Be not afraid, what e'er betide / God will take care of you," I hear my mother's voice. As a child I heard hymns in church and song in the woods, in the trees, among the grasses, and sometimes from the rocks.

My father's father was a miner. My father was a mining engineer who went to university at a land-grant school on the basis of his keen intelligence, his own work in the mines, and, for his master's degree, the G.I. Bill after World War II. He loved mining and miners. He loved what he did for a living. My formative years were spent in the mountains where little "coal camps" like Goodwill or Epperly (where we lived and which no longer exist) were perched on the hills or tucked into the "hollers," the little valleys between mountains from which there is no exit "on the other end." I was born in the hospital in Bluefield, a town half in Virginia (which represented the Old South and aristocracy, mother's father's people) and half in West Virginia (which represented mountain people, Daddy's people). I am a "border person" by geography and family background, a cross between aristocratic Easterners and the pioneers who in the eighteenth century settled in the "western mountains." I carry the blue blood of Richmond and that of Daniel Boone's associates in my veins. Sometimes I don't know who I am.

In my early years I was left alone with my own imagination, a terrific swing outside the kitchen window (in mother's sight), a *not* AKC-registered English setter called "True Girl," and the Presence and presences that inhabit the hills and woods. So I didn't get on too well when we moved into the county seat for me to start school and for my brother to be born. He's a town boy; I'm a mountain girl. To say I had few "people skills" is a kindness. I never felt I "fit in" or could quite figure out what was going on. I hid in my books and my head, except for the glorious two weeks every summer at Girl Scout Camp when I lived in a tent in the woods and sang around the campfire at night. Bliss. I was an obedient child (most of the time!), a good student, an early reader, and "pious." This last came naturally too.

My mother's father was a Campbellite evangelist. He and my grandmother went into a community, and he preached up a congregation. My grandmother played the organ and said she built the church buildings on her donut recipe. My mother moved a *lot* during her childhood. She really believed the principles of Alexander and Thomas Campbell, founders of what was in the nineteenth century America's largest indigenous Christian denomination. Not for us the local Methodist chapel (Dad's family heritage). Before we moved, every Sunday we drove the winding mountain roads into town to the First Christian Church. Among my first memories are my father's baptism (immersion) there and my imposing paternal grandfather being called on to give the benediction after church services when he visited. At least until the time I went to college (our *church's* college, naturally), when the church doors were open, we were probably there. I *liked* church (mostly). I certainly liked (and read) the Bible I and every other child was given at the end of third grade Sunday School. I owe that church a lot.

So what does all this have to do with these poems? I hope it helps explain why I would be deeply moved by and led to write about the people and places from which my kinfolk came. In his book *Journeys on the Edge: The Celtic Tradition*, Thomas O'Loughlin says, ". . . we know better where we are today if we know our place's past."[1] I would add, "if we know our people's past." *Pace* New Criticism, you will know this book better when you know how I am connected to place, people, faith: English and Celtic peoples spiritually influenced by renegades from Scots

1. Thomas O'Loughlin, *Journeys on the Edge: The Celtic Tradition* (Maryknoll, NY: Orbis Press, 2000), 29.

Presbyterianism and the Established Church. Fast forward to the late 1990s when I began to have various bits of work to do in the United Kingdom. (I had spent part of my junior year in college at Oxford but was too busy turning twenty to notice much.) As a guest of the Thomas Merton Society of Great Britain and Ireland, I met Esther de Waal who became a friend and generous promoter of my poetry. She introduced me to most of the people to whom this book is dedicated.

When I first visited Esther on the borders between England and Wales—that mystical land of the Black Mountains, the Skirrid, the Hill of the Angels, the Golden Valley, the Wye Valley—I felt at *home*. I can't explain it exactly, but I *belonged* there. I had a similar experience when I visited Iona, the holy island that is a spiritual home to so many. Later, quite by chance, I discovered that my father's mother's people are descended from one Thomas Morris, who was born in the early eighteenth century in Wales and who, family legend has it, came to America as a stowaway. Celtic lands and peoples got into my blood because they were already in my blood. In the bardic tradition of the lands of my ancestors, I *had* to "sing" about it.

The following poems depict the effect on me of person and place. The collection falls into two parts. Part 1 consists of poetic meditations on Celtic saints. Readers of a certain age might be reminded of Helen Waddell's lovely little book *Beasts and Saints*.[2] Part 2, the longer section, is made up of sequences of poems

2. Helen Waddell, trans., *Beasts and Saints* (London: Constable and Company, Ltd., 1934/53). The woodcuts by Robert Gibbings contribute to the charm of the book. It has been reissued with an introduction by Esther de Waal (London: Darton, Longman and Todd, 1995; Grand Rapids, MI: Wm. B. Eerdmans Publishing Co., 1996).

about places: Iona, Herefordshire and the Welsh borders, Wales itself, and finally the Anglican convent of Tymawr in Wales, a living continuity with the tradition of Celtic Christianity. If there's anything different about my approach to the Celtic it's that it doesn't focus on Ireland, in America, at least, the best known of the Celtic lands.

In a roundabout way, by reading these poems you're reading my autobiography. It's an overflowing of my heart's response to being in places from which my family came. It's the understandable response of somebody raised close to the natural world, in mountains full of mystery and presences. And, in the interest of full disclosure, the historical "framing" of the poems in the essays and notes is the natural response of a scholar to a lot of popular rubbish that passes itself off as "Celtic spirituality." I hope the brief introductions and the notes for some of the poems will help "place" for you the saints and locations about which the poems speak. If the pedantic apparatus annoys or distracts you, ignore it. Prefaces are skipable; notes are easily ignored.

Finally, this little collection is a thank-you gift to the "new friends" among whom I instantly felt belonging when I first met them. Perhaps what I've revealed explains why that belonging was so monumentally important. After having been for many years in the public role of scholar/pedant, they recognized and affirmed the "private person" who, since childhood, had been a poet. In middle age, that encouragement has meant everything. It has given me my voice.

So my deepest gratitude to the "border friends" who have offered me lavish "heart hospitality": Esther; Christine and Tony; Nora and Michael (who published my first two collections of verse); Stevie and James and Bertie; Leah and Robert (whose hearts are in the borders); the community of St. Peter's Church, Rowlestone, especially Elizabeth; Fr. Dennis (St. Dennis of Monger); accomplished and extraordinary Welsh poets Ruth and Anne; the community (living and heavenly) around the Society of the Sacred Cross, Tymawr Convent, the sisters, Br. Jack, Andrea, and Agnes. This book is for you as

> I am giving my heart
> to the land and its creatures.
> I am giving my heart
> to the land's beloved ones.
> I am giving my heart
> to the God of the land,
> the creatures, the beloved.

Once, after doing the dishes, as we stood at the big kitchen window watching the rain lash Tymawr's extraordinary trees, after he'd said in his gorgeous Scots, "Lovely weather, isn't it?" Br. Jack asked me, "When the scholar and the poet wrestles in you, who wins?" You read the book and decide.

The Anchorage
Wheeling, West Virginia, USA
March 1, 2009, St. David's Day

Part I

Celtic Saints

Celtic Culdees

After the silent centuries I weave their praise.
The core of faith is one and it is splendid to know
Souls that are one with the quick in the root of Being.

—*Dail Pren*, Waldo Williams

I praise these martyrs,
red, white, or green.
I praise these martyrs,
and the God they've seen.

"Culdee" has been described as "the most abused term in Scotic [*sic*] church history." According to Richard Sharpe in his introduction to Adomnan's *Life of St. Columba*, it derives from the Irish *celi De*, "client of God" or "companion of God," and is used for religious who "sought a more devout life within or apart from the large monastic centres in ninth century Ireland" (London: Penguin Books, 1995). It has had many uses (and abuses), but I use it here to mean simply "friend of God."

An earlier and briefer version of this sequence of poems appeared in my small collection *The Heart's Lands* (Abergavenny, Wales: Three Peaks Press, 2001). It is now out of print, but I am grateful to its original publisher, Michael Woodward, both for that edition and for permission to reproduce poems in this one.

In this edition (and in subsequent sections of poems herein), +++ marks a division between poems on the same subject or in the same sequence.

Celtic tradition has at least three forms of martyrdom: red, the spilling of blood, giving one's life for Christ; white, exile from all that one loves, journeying with no specific destination in mind; green, the martyrdom of penance and repentance, often manifested externally in anchoritic (hermit) life. See Esther de Waal, *The Celtic Way of Prayer: The Recovery of the Religious Imagination* (New York: Doubleday, 1997; Norwich: Canterbury Press, 2011 [2nd ed.]), chaps. 1 and 6; and Philip Sheldrake, *Living Between Worlds* (Cambridge, MA: Cowley Publications, 1996), chap. 5.

I

Patrick

What shall we say of Patrick
the quintessential Irishman
who wasn't?

Son of a British deacon
who was son of a priest,
you were stolen by pirates,
enslaved in Ireland.
For six long years
you tended sheep,
then went home
on the strength of a dream.

You trained in Gaul,
took up the family business,
then the Dream-Maker
called you back
to bitter Ireland
to pastor His flock,
to teach His people,
to be an icon of forgiveness.

Dare we believe the stories
of serpents and shamrocks,
of Druids silenced at Tara?
Dare we believe your prayer
that God the Three-in-One,

the strength of all dreamers,
is before and behind,
above, below, and with us?

Patrick, be our breastplate.
Stand between us
and the darkness.

St. Patrick (390–461) is the best known of the Celtic saints. He was born in what is now England and at sixteen was carried to Ireland by slave raiders. Six years later he escaped and returned home, where a dream indicated that he must return to Ireland as a missionary. He trained for the priesthood in Gaul, returning to Ireland in 432. He established the episcopal see in Armagh in 444. There are many famous (and apocryphal!) stories about Patrick: how he silenced the Druids in Tara, drove the serpents out of Ireland, used a shamrock to explain the Trinity. Embodiment of the missionary spirit of Celtic Christianity, his feast day is March 17.

II

Brigid of Kildare

Brigid shares her fertile feast
with a Druid goddess.
She, like the church
in her land,
is wedded to something
older than Christ.

Mary of the Gael
called women to Kildare
to community,
a city of the poor,
with fire at its heart,
fire not to be put out.

When he raised his hand
to bless her nun's vows,
the Bishop Mel saw
tongues of fire on her head,
fire which took his tongue,
for he spoke her bishop.

Brigid of untameable goodness,
who sold the sword for the poor,
who drove the devil back
with a cross of straw,
Brigid, who wears a miter of fire,
may your tribe increase.

+++

Bridget, Bride, Ffraid
beloved of Irish, Scots, Welsh,
daughter of Druid
she gave milk to beggars,
sight to blind,
tamed a wolf for a chief
and Imbolg for the Christ.
His fearless Bride
stands wrapped in white mantle
before the crimson altar
of their oak church
with a cross of straw
and a bowl of fire
to hold back the devil
and the darkness,
to give us reason to hope.

Brigid (d. 525) was not just from Kildare ("Church of the Oak"). She is known in Scotland as Bride, in Wales as Ffraid. In one story she gave her warrior father's sword to a beggar. A woman of great compassion, hospitality, and generosity, she is best known as the founder of a religious community at Kildare, which was for a time the largest settlement in Ireland and known as "the city of the poor." Her mythology ties her to a Druid fertility goddess and also suggests she was miraculously made a bishop. She is reported to have said, "Since my mind was once set on God, it never departed from Him." Her feast day is February 1.

The story of her life is beautifully told in Welsh poet Ruth Bidgood's "Hymn to Sant [*sic*] Ffraid," originally commissioned by BBC Radio Wales and broadcast 5 April 1979. It appears in her collection *Symbols of Plenty* (Norwich: Canterbury Press, 2006).

In "pagan reckoning," Imbolg, February 1, was a "quarter day," halfway between the solstice and the equinox. Its imagery became part of the Brigid traditions, and one cannot help but note that the feast of Candlemas has been set on the next day, February 2.

III

Illtud

Illtud, son of Cassian's house,
made his own in Wales
a center for study,
a home for art.

Llanilltyd grew
and consumed its land.
So Illtud took his staff,
drew a line in the sand
and forbade the sea to cross.

Illtud, whom the sea obeyed,
withdrew to a lonely place to pray,
and crossed the sea to Brittany,
a pilgrim known
for all he knew.

Most learned
of all the Britons,
teach us, Illtud,
where to draw the line.

A fifth- or sixth-century Welsh saint, Illtud was the abbot of a large monastery. He was known for his great learning and for his miracles. A twelfth-century life of Illtud says he came originally from Brittany. His feast is November 6.

John Cassian (ca. 360–430), the great monastic founder and theologian, was much influenced by Evagrius Ponticus and himself greatly influenced St. Benedict. In the Eastern Church his feast day is February 29.

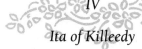

IV

Ita of Killeedy

Mother Ita,
your nuns at Limerick
taught boys like Brendan.
Was it you who made them
so restless for God
that they sailed small ships
to the edge of the sea?
Was the hard life
you chose for yourself,
martyrdom's green way,
meant to slake
that selfsame thirst
which, being woman,
you could not quench
by voyaging?

In the sixth century Ita was head of a community of women in County Limerick which had a respected school for boys. The legends around her stress her austere life and her miracles. Her feast day is January 15.

V

David of Wales

Dewi, the saint maker,
patron of Welshmen
(fierce warriors
who sing like angels)
was one of them.

White martyr,
he wandered from Wales,
to the City of God,
in holy Zion
was given his chair,
returned home primate,
built twelve houses
known for their harshness,
gave his name
to fifty places,
and when he preached
the earth itself
rose up beneath his feet
so all could see
and hear the Waterman
tell of the ways of God.

Dewi, saint maker,
make of our soldiers singers.
Our mountains will sing with them,
and all the trees of the forest
will clap their hands.

St. David (Dewi, d. ca. 547) is the patron saint of Wales. Son of a Cardigan chieftain, he founded twelve monasteries and made a pilgrimage to Jerusalem where he was consecrated bishop. He lived a strict monastic life and was known as the "Waterman," perhaps because he was a teetotaler. There is a legend that as he was preaching a mound grew up under his feet so that his congregation could better see and hear him. His influence was such that he is sometimes called "the saint maker." His feast day is March 1. For more on St. David see the subsequent section of Welsh poems in this collection.

VI

Brendan the Navigator

He founded a house,
but hungered for homelessness.
To arrive was his snare,
to journey, his freedom.

He sought the sea's rootlessness,
peregrinatio por Dei amore,
sailed his curach from Cork
to discover his desert
in pathless waters.

He voyaged
into the unknown,
to find the Land of Promise,
to show us the way Home.

St. Brendan (d. 575) is representative of the Celtic tradition of pilgrimage. Born in Kerry, he was one of the children cared for by St. Ita at Killeedy. He founded the monastery at Clonfert, Galway ca. 560. Brendan and fourteen companions set out in small boats without sails in order to let God direct their travels. (See note on p. 3 on white martyrdom.) The tenth-century tale of Brendan's voyage says he sailed to the "Beautiful Land of Promise," perhaps the Canary Islands or North America. I have heard of mysterious and genuine Celtic runes in a cave in the mountains near where I grew up in West Virginia attributed to Brendan. His feast day is May 16, and his story is well told in Frederick Beuchner's novel *Brendan* (San Francisco: Harper & Row, 1988).

peregrinatio por Dei amore: A traveler or journeyer for the love of God.

VII

Columba of Iona

The Dove flew
to a place of water,
wind, and rock,
a place beyond
sight of home,
out at earth's edge,
out where the sea drops off
into empty air.

The Dove knew
we always stand
facing the end
which makes now
sweet, full
and fragile.

+++

St. Columba Speaks

I was blown
from an isle in the sea
to a rock in the sea,
martyr to murder
I may not have done.
Some nights I see
the heavens on fire.

Some days I feel
like the broken shells
I find far inland,
shattered on stone,
sucked dry by birds.
Some days I feel
hearty as heather
and as deeply rooted,
full of the spirit
of this pulsating place,
one with its winds.
They can blow in
from homeward West,
bring a stalking fog,
greedy, gray beast
that devours the sea,
the rock, the past.
Like St. Paul,
I press on.

+++

9 June A.D. 597

Exiled Columba preached, baptized,
studied, wrote, and governed.
From his tiny island
rose a mighty alleluia
to the Lord of exiles, scholars,
those who travel for truth.
Some Scots sing it still.

Beyond his three score and ten,
he lived in scriptorium and psalter.
After copying texts,
on the night of his *transitus*
he went smiling to the abbey's
great, green altar. Before Matins
the angels gathered him up
in heaven's light embrace.

Over Iona, they brightened the sky.
Fishermen in the river Finn
saw a pillar of flame.
After his death, for three days
the wind lashed the waters.
Then there was a mighty calm.
Columba's exile had ended.

Columba (d. 597) or Colmcille (the dove) was an Irishman who left Ireland as an act of both white and green martyrdom after a battle for which he felt he had some responsibility. With twelve companions, he landed on Iona in the spring of 563, from which he could not even see his home in Ireland. He is said to have driven a monster from the River Ness with the sign of the Cross. He made four monastic settlements in Scotland, the most famous and influential of which was Iona. (See the subsequent sequence of Iona poems.) Columba was known for his diplomatic gifts, his extraordinary life of prayer, and especially for "second sight," a sort of prescience that is still evident among Scots-Irish southern mountain people. His fellow monk of Iona, Adomnan, wrote his life a century after his death. It reads well even today and is readily available in a translation by Richard Sharpe (London: Penguin Books, 1995). Columba's feast is June 9.

The date is that of Columba's death. The poem is *in memoriam* for Jim Hughes, a latter-day son of Iona, now watching over that holy place from "the farther shore and the greater light."

VIII

Kentigern of Glasgow

From inauspicious birth
you became Glasgow's
most dear shepherd,
then a white martyr.

Exiled from your chair,
beloved of the Dove,
patron of the fallen,
soul-son of Magdalene
who loved much,
guide us gently
with your staff.
Prod us lest we fall.

Also known as St. Mungo, Kentigern was a missionary in Scotland, became bishop of the Britons of Strathclyde, and founded the church in Glasgow. He preached in Wales and Cumbria but was buried c. 612 in Glasgow. One can see his tomb in the cathedral there. His feast day is January 13.

IX

Kevin

Monks taught you,
but you did not dwell
with your brothers,
went the hermit's way,
prayed alone.

A blackbird
laid her eggs
in your hand.
You held them
until they hatched,
her whole world
in your hands.

The heaven's are God's;
the earth God gives us.
Teach us to love this world,
to hold its eggs gently
and when they hatch
to open our hands
and glory in their flight.

Kevin (d. 618) was educated by monks, but following the pattern of so many Celtic saints, chose to become a hermit. He founded the monastery at Glendalough before becoming a hermit. He had a keen feeling for nature and many of the stories about him focus on his affinity for God's creatures. The most famous is the story of the blackbird's nest. His feast day is June 3.

X

Aidan of Lindisfarne

Like as the hart
longeth for the water,
you with your twelve
fled like a stag
from the home of the Dove
to an isle in the sea
and made of its rock
a cradle of Christianity.

Your house put its wealth
at the feet of the poor.
Your isle is called holy;
it gave up its store.

Aidan (d. 651) was born in Ireland and, for a time, was a monk of Iona. With twelve companions he evangelized northern England and founded the monastery at Lindisfarne, the Holy Island, which twice a day is cut off from the mainland by the tides. Contrary to common practice, Aidan allowed no wealth to accumulate at his monastery, instead giving any surplus to the poor. His emblem is the stag. (The white stag is sometimes used as a symbol for Christ.) His feast day is August 31.

XI

Hilda of Whitby

Of noble birth,
christened by a saint,
she became a nun,
abbess of a double house.
She wrote its rule,
insisted Scripture be studied,
mothered arts and learning,
nurtured Caedmon
who first hymned
heaven-kingdom's Guardian
in our native tongue.

In 664
she opened her door
because she knew
the rune of hospitality.
She kept it to the letter,
And it spelled the doom
of her way of life.

Author of "Caedmon's Hymn," one of the, if not the, earliest English poems.

Celtic Christianity is not short on strong women! The grandniece of King Edmund, and of noble parentage, Hilda (d. 680) was brought to Christ by St. Paulinus at York in 627 when she was thirteen. Much later she became a nun and was made abbess in 649 by St. Aidan. She founded a double monastery (one that had both women and men) at Whitby which was a great center of arts and learning, especially the study of Scripture. Perhaps because Hilda was renowned as a peacemaker, her community hosted the famous Synod of Whitby in 664. Her feast day is November 17.

XII

Cuthbert

Cuthbert the shepherd
while tending sheep
saw heaven open
and the heavenly hosts
welcome the bright spirit
of blessed Aidan.
So he got him
to a monastery
and went from tending sheep
to tending sheep.

+++

He began tending sheep,
in a vision of light
saw angels carrying
souls to heaven.

Melrose made
the shepherd a monk,
and the monk, a pastor,
an itinerant servant of souls.

Lindisfarne made
the pastor a prior
whose heart longed
for an anchor-hold.

He found it at Farne.
But the Church
called the hermit
to shepherd its souls,

and when the bishop died
moved his obedient bones
from the Holy Isle
to the cathedral he'd fled.

Poor, strong Cuthbert
gave so much
and got so little,
not even a quiet tomb.

While tending sheep, Cuthbert (d. 687), a Northumbrian Englishman, had a vision of light in which angels were carrying souls to heaven. (Columba had similar visions.) He became a monk at Melrose and was later prior at Lindisfarne. In 676 he retired to Farne until in 684 he was called to be bishop of Hexham. He was buried at Lindisfarne, but his remains were later moved to Durham. He is known for his physical prowess, his close observation of nature, and his miracles. His feast day is March 20.

The Celtic Culdees

It wasn't Rome
brought their demise
(though prelates
tell the tale thus),
but Viking raiders
killed and took
them captive,
carried away
what little they had.

These dear martyrs,
companions of God,
are not gone
who faithfully left
illuminated maps
of the heart's lands,
stone churches,
high crosses,
the call of anchor-hold,
the lure of pilgrimage,
the challenge to see,
if only in mirror darkly,
creation charged
with the glory of heaven
and God's hand
guiding our wee curach
to the harbor home
of heaven's host.

Part II

Celtic Places

Iona

Thanks to the extraordinary work of George F. MacLeod and the Iona Community this tiny Hebridean island again exerts a mighty influence on Christianity. It has already been introduced in this book in reference to several of the Celtic saints, and especially Columba who, after the Battle of Cieldrebene in 561 for which he felt partially responsible, undertook the white martyrdom of exile from his beloved Ireland. In 563 with his companions he sailed as "pilgrim for Christ" to Iona where he founded a monastery whose influence extended to most of Western Christendom for several centuries. Columba's story and that of Iona's founding was charmingly told by a later abbot, Adomnan, who, writing in Latin in the seventh century produced perhaps the most complete biography written in Europe at the time.[1] Closing his study of Celtic spirituality with a chapter on Iona, Philip Sheldrake notes that the "community Columba founded there was not only the direct ancestor of much of the Christian Church in Scotland; through its daughter settlement on the island

---

1. It is easily available in a good modern edition: Adomnan of Iona, *Life of St. Columba*, trans. Richard Sharpe (London: Penguin Books, 1995).

of Lindisfarne (or Holy Island) Iona was also indirectly the source of Christianity in northern England."[2]

Beginning in the 790s Iona (and other Celtic monasteries) was the target of vicious Viking attacks. For a while the community was scattered. In 1203 the abbey was reorganized under Benedictine rule and an Augustinian nunnery was founded nearby. In 1499 the abbey was acquired by the Scottish bishops, and after the Reformation in the seventeenth century it fell into disrepair. Of his eighteenth-century visit there Samuel Johnson writes, "The Island, which was once the metropolis of learning and piety, has now no school for education nor temple for worship, only two inhabitants that can speak *English*, and not one that can read or write."[3] Nevertheless, Boswell's journal records Johnson saying, "That man is little to be envied, whose patriotism would not gain force upon the plain of *Marathon*, or whose piety would not grow warmer among the ruins of *Iona!*"[4] (Italics in the originals.) The Duke of Argyll who owned the land gave the ruins to the Church of Scotland in 1899 which restored and reroofed it between 1902 and 1911. Enter George F. MacLeod (1895–1991).

MacLeod was educated at Winchester College and read law at Oriel College in Oxford before the First World War. He enlisted in 1914 and suffered the horrors and dislocation of so many of his generation. After the war he trained for the ministry at Edinburgh University and, from a fashionable

---

2. Philip Sheldrake, *Living Between Worlds: Place and Journey in Celtic Spirituality* (Boston: Cowley Publications, 1996), 83.

3. Allan Wendt, ed., *Johnson's Journey to the Western Islands* (1775) and *Boswell's Journal of a Tour to the Hebrides* (1785) (Boston: Houghton Mifflin, 1965), 113.

4. Boswell in Wendt, ed., 335.

Edinburgh parish, moved to the slums of Glasgow in 1930. For the rest of his life he remained a major voice for social justice. His public accomplishments were impressive (he was chaplain to the queen in 1956, moderator of the Church of Scotland in 1957, sat in the House of Lords, and was president of the International Fellowship of Reconciliation in 1967) and include founding of the Iona Community in 1938. The Iona Community continues as an ecumenical Christian body devoted to worship, contemplation, and social action.[5] Since 1952 it has been affiliated with the Church of Scotland but is open to all Christians. Between 1938 and 1967 the medieval abbey church and many surrounding buildings have been restored by the Cathedral Trustees through Iona Abbey Ltd. and the work of Iona Community members. A touching piece of that story is that after World War II Norway made a major gift of timber for its reconstruction as an apology for what the Vikings had done a thousand years earlier.

The Iona community was founded to deepen prayer and social action and the connection between the two. In the process it has made major contributions to the development of ecumenical liturgies and to church music. Members of the community, who now stretch across the globe, commit themselves to a discipline of prayer and Bible study, meeting together (community), accountability for use of time and money, and work for peace and justice. Many spend three months on Iona in preparation for work in industrial areas, poor communities, or political action. Today visitors to tiny, remote Iona (estimated at one hundred thousand

5. For more information and relevant contacts see www.iona.org.uk and the publication arm of the Iona Community, Wild Goose Publications.

annually) find a place of inclusiveness, spiritual healing, and political activity for justice.[6]

On Wednesdays anyone on Iona who cares to do so may join a pilgrimage that walks to places of historic and spiritual interest. It begins by the abbey church at the foot of St. Martin's Cross and ends at St. Oran's Chapel, the oldest continually used structure in the monastic complex. Pilgrims make their way from St. Martin's Cross to the ruins of the Augustinian nunnery, through the marble quarry with its distinctive green stone (of which the great abbey altar is constructed), and on to St. Columba's Bay, the southern tip of the island where Columba first landed. Then the way leads north through the Machair ("raised beach" which has been for centuries farm fields) to the Hermit's Cell, perhaps up Dun I (at 102 meters above sea level, the highest point on the island) with its mysterious spring of water, and then back to the abbey and St. Oran's Chapel which, from the ninth century, was the burial place of Scottish kings. The following sequence of poems takes you to Iona and on this pilgrimage.[7]

6. For more on the recent history of Iona see J. Philip Newell, *Listening for the Heartbeat of God: A Celtic Spirituality* (New York: Paulist Press, 1997).

7. For a description of the Iona Pilgrimage see *The Iona Community Worship Book* (Glasgow: Wild Goose Publications, 1994). I have used the third edition.

The Iona Sequence

The angel of the LORD found her by a spring of water in
the wilderness. . . . And he said, ". . . where have
you come from and where are you going?"

Genesis 16:7-8 (NRSV)

In Pursuit of Christ the Deer

It was no white stag,
and I drew back no royal arrow,
but glimpsed in Mull's bracken
the noble head and rack
of a great, wild stag
which vanished behind a rock
as if he had never been.

It was, in this, like Holyrood's founding:
Revelation of Christ's hiddenness,
Who shows a fleeting face
then melts into impenetrability
leaving my soul as a hart,
longing for living water,
athirst for a living God.

It is a full day's journey from Glasgow to Iona overland via Oban, where one takes a ferry to the Isle of Mull, crosses Mull by coach/bus and then takes another ferry to Iona. There is a tradition that Holyrood (Holy Cross) Palace in Edinburgh was founded when St. Margaret's son, David, was hunting and encountered a great white stag with a golden cross on its forehead. He understood the stag to be the Christ.

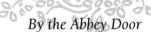

By the Abbey Door

By the abbey door
for the Celtic Ibn Sabeel,
a stone encircled well,
an offering of water.

By the abbey door
for the weary traveler,
an ancient stone foot bath,
an offering of hospitality.

By the abbey door
for the wandering heart
a stone base missing its cross,
an offering of absence.

Beyond the abbey door
a small stone in an expansive sea
offering expansiveness,
wordlessness, wind.

In Islamic tradition the "Ibn Sabeel," the "son of the fountain," is one so poor he only has the free water at the mosque. Thus he is an image of perfect submission to and dependence on God.

St. Columba's Shrine

The language at holy places
can overwhelm.
It washes over,
threatens to swamp.
When a place is prayer
words are extraneous.

From the brilliant light
of island summer,
crowds of visitors,
the liturgy itself,
I bow to enter
your simple shrine.

Affixed to the abbey's facade,
often mysteriously invisible
to touring passersby,
its simple arched door
offers subtle invitation
to smallness, shadow, silence.

St. Martin's Cross

It begins and ends here
with Martin who forswore the sword,
disliked the Chair to which he was obedient,
was gentle with heretics, loved hermitage,
took the cross to the Celts.

The shadow of the cross comforts
scars medieval cart wheels
cut in rough, rosy stones
that mark this sacred way.
Street of the Dead, Road of Kings:

two names for the same journey.
In this pilgrim life
we are royal in our dying,
rest grateful heads on the cross,
feel its blessed benediction.

The Martin is Martin of Tours (d. 397), patron of France, the soldier who had a vision of
Christ after which he joined St. Hilary at Poitiers. He praised and practiced the monastic
way and spent part of his life as a hermit.

Anna MacClean, d. 1543

There on her stone slab
stands Anna MacClean
Augustianian prioress,
her hands, like her drapery,
eternally pious in prayer.
Around her head
a flock of angels hover.

What was her life like
as Reform swirled furiously
toward her tiny island
like Viking hoards of old?
Her nunnery walls fell,
broke open her silent tomb,
but left her memory
crowned with angels.

The stone slab that marked the tomb of Augustinian prioress Anna MacClean is on display in
the museum behind Iona Abbey. The ruins of her nunnery are extensive and clearly marked,
giving the visitor a sense of the "shape" of a monastic community.

St. Columba's Bay

We did not come
in little leather boats
but from a heather crowned hill,
through a marsh of yellow flag.
St. Columba's Bay at high noon
is leaden with the grief
of leaving behind,
alive with the energy
of an uncertain future.
Here begins the journey
to an unknown home.

Landward arrival presents the choice
that makes all the difference:
go to the wide, grassy left
or the narrow, rocky right
where sea and stone
sing a *sotto voce* duet,
a rhythmic reminder that
life is a call to renounce and embrace,
the reason for pilgrimage,
like that for creation,
is to rise from the dead.

Hermit's Cell

In a green glen
surrounded by great, gray rock,
open to the sight of the sea
and its eternal invitation,
all that remains of the hermit's cell
(if that is what it was)
is the base of a beehive hut,
foundation of a solitary life
that whispers across the ages,
"be still and know."

To sit in its circle of stone
is to enter ascending energy,
urgent a millennia after
the last hermit left,
surely lifted up
on a swirling wind of fire.

Dun I

From the highest point
the mountaintop vision:
natural beauty of islands,
Cuillins of Skye, Paps of Jura,
Staffa's dark cave,
the outline of eternity etched
in the white martyrdom of islands,
the red martyrdom of a white beach
where monks were murdered
when death sailed in on the sea.

Behind history's stark juxtapositions
the wind murmurs God's call to Abram,
"Raise your eyes and look
from the place where you are."

At 102 meters above sea level, Dun I (pronounced "Dun-E") is the highest point on Iona.
Looking northeast, one sees a beautiful sandy white beach where Vikings killed some
eighty monks.

Fountain of Eternal Youth

Just below the summit,
a coming down place,
primitive, primeval place
whose brackish waters promise
the vain desire of the ages:
eternal youth.

What fool wants it?
We are dust-formed creatures
products of divinely planned obsolescence,
made for the process of divestment,
the challenge of gently letting go.
Without death, there is no rising.

I take in the power of the place,
not desiring youth, do not drink,
but sign my head to remember,
look up, see two barefoot nymphs
wearing rock star T-shirts,
weaving Bridget's crosses of straw.

St. Oran's Chapel

In the oldest place
where kings are buried
the oldest woman,

bent and staggering,
fell onto the rickety back bench.
Bowed head, shoulders hunched,
face in hands, pink scalp
visible through thin, white hair,
she prayed and prayed and prayed.

Then, abruptly, with youthful vigor,
sat up, said aloud, "Yes!"
rested peacefully a while longer,
after several minutes struggled up
chanting under her breath,
"yes, yes, yes."

In the oldest place
where commoners are resurrected,
the holiest word.

Epitaph: St. Oran's Yard

In a slightly overgrown corner
of St. Oran's burial ground
a newer stone protects
a more recent occupant:
"A sailor of the 1939–1945 war
Found October 14, 1940."

To the good island folk
who live facing sunset,
the sea returned a body
unknown but by bits
of unrotted uniform:
"Merchant Marine."

An anonymous mariner,
noncombatant in a terrible war,
who died alone in the Atlantic
was embraced by strangers
who knew him some mother's son,
was buried in holy shadow
with the kings of western isles,
and is "Known to God."

High Crosses

Not in darkened nave,
nor displaying a dying man,
they stand under open skies,
gray eminences over green lands.

These sacred trees connect
earth and heaven, matter and air.
All God's good creatures
shelter in their shadow.

The orb of the Druid becomes
a halo of stone around Christ
triumphant at the center,
life-liberating axis of everything.

Norsemen should have known
people who carve their Christ in stone
are rooted as rock,
intend to stay no matter what.

St. Columba's Pillow

It rests beneath an iron cage
in an obscure corner,
an unremarkable ovoid stone.

When Columba put down his prayers,
gave up his cross vigil,
laid his blessed head
on uncompromising hardness,
did he dream dreams
of angels ascending and descending,
know God had given him
this living, holy land?

Does the Dove who sleeps on a stone
know himself at the gate of heaven,
know every place and moment is Bethel?

Wind, Water, Rock

Iona's holiness and healing
is in the confluence of elemental things,
the wind that gathers primeval waters;
the waters from which life came;
the life that, like summer solstice
light, glows at midnight;
the rock that gives substance, solidity,
a place for permanent belonging.
And over it all, the birds swirl
hurling down the blessing of song.

Heretofore becalmed by demons,
amid these vibratory presences
they disperse, limp, and scrabble away,
and, in my darkness, a wind begins to stir.

Wind Holds

Only the sharpest wind
clears away enveloping fog.

On the blusteriest days
the wind holds gulls
suspended on shelves of air.

Spreading unresisting wings,
they float on fiercest gales,
submit to what might be
storm's clarifying wisdom.

Flowering Place

For all its rock and wind
Iona is a flowering place.
Fuchsia hedges mark
gardens of Russian iris,
spikes of foxglove bells,
waving lavender wands.
The meadows are mottled
with minute daisies, buttercups.
The petals of purple stars,
golden stamen thin as thread,
explode in clusters
from unyielding granite walls.
Most amazing of all
from the earthless shingle
of St. Columba's Bay
low-lying yellow flowers,
spiny leaves to prick gull's tongue,
strain sunward through stone.

When he arrived in his tiny boat,
faced the barren hills
with who knows what behind,
was the saint, too, welcomed
by this field of yellow flag,
only three in bloom,
not knowing whether
they had been or were coming?

The Christ of Iona

The Christ of Iona
is the rock of ages,
stark solidity of elemental things.

The Christ of Iona
is the mirror-still sea,
the green giving life rain's lashing.

The Christ of Iona
is the wild wind
on the highlands' barren faces.

The Christ of Iona
is blazing fire,
summer solstice sun.

The Christ of Iona
is night's impenetrable darkness,
the mystery of unknowing.

The Christ of Iona
is the sea birds'
freedom of flight.

The Christ of Iona
is lupine, yellow flag, foxglove,
the gratuitous color of creation.

The Christ of Iona
came from creation's God
welcoming arms already extended.

The Christ of Iona
rises repeatedly to break open
life's cosmic, fecundating egg.

Passing Places

On narrow reticulating roads
that thread their way
through the green moonscape
of the highlands' severe loveliness
the occasional widenings
are signed "passing place."

Engulfed in elemental beauty
searing in its intensity,
that peels the callous heart
as if it were Eve's apple,
I know, oh I know,
they all are. They all are.

Herefordshire and the Welsh Borders[1]

Any number of writers and scholars note that being geographi-
cally on the "edge," or "between worlds," or in "border lands"
both characterizes and has had a profound effect on identity and
spirituality.[2] Thomas O'Loughlin, in a chapter titled "Living on
the Fringes," suggests that the Celtic Christians were "on the
edge," necessitating the "need to shout one's identity," to tell those
closer to the "center" not to forget those on the fringe. "People
who live at the heart of affairs," he writes, "have a tendency to
forget those out in the surrounding land."[3] Living on what was
at my country's founding the border between east and west, and
is still that between north and south, my experience as an Appalachian American confirms the truth of this assertion. Such is
the burden and joy of border people: being forgotten and being

---

1. Some of these poems first appeared in my collection *The Heart's Lands*
(Abergavenny, Wales: Three Peaks Press, 2001) now long out of print and used
by the kind permission of Michael Woodward, the original editor and publisher.

2. See, for example, Esther de Waal, *Living on the Border: Connecting Inner
and Outer Worlds* (Norwich, England: Canterbury Press, 2001; new enlarged
edition with illustrations and anthology, 2011); and *To Pause at the Threshold:
Reflections on Living on the Border* (Harrisburg, PA: Morehouse Publishing, 2001);
Thomas O'Loughlin, *Journeys on the Edge: The Celtic Tradition* (Maryknoll, NY:
Orbis Press, 2000); Philip Sheldrake, *Living Between Worlds* (Boston: Cowley
Publications, 1996).

3. O'Loughlin, *Journeys on the Edge*, 50.

forgotten. Tracing the Celtic Christian tradition east from the British Isles, one remembers that Brittany is the western border of the European continent, just as Wales is the western edge of the British Isle and Ireland is of all of Europe as it faces the setting sun, what was in the Middle Ages the darkness of the unknown. Perhaps "there be dragons."

The particular border area that the following poem sequence describes is the border between what is now England and Wales. For centuries it was contested territory. Technically, I suppose, if you drew a line from Chester, England, south to Newport, Wales, the territory along and west of the line is the country I have in mind. It includes, of course, the medieval monastic center of Shrewsbury popularized by Ellis Peters' wonderful Brother Cadfael mystery series. The specific area treated by these poems is the area around Hereford, with the great cathedral's chained library and medieval "Mappa Mundi," more specifically still, the area between the Wye River and the Black Mountains, mostly Herefordshire, but including bits of Monmouthshire and the area north of Brecon in Wales. It includes the "Marches" and is dominated by the Black Mountains and the Valleys of the Wye and Monnow Rivers. It is the area so charmingly written about by the Rev. Francis Kilvert in the nineteenth century. His diary is still one of the best introductions to the area.

I believe if one is fortunate enough to be born to a landscape and belong to a place, that landscape shapes the person's perception of God. I once heard Esther de Waal say, "the land has its own vocabulary."[4] The language those letters write in these

4. Lecture at the Cathedral College of the Washington National Cathedral, Washington, DC, February 3, 2009.

particular borders stretches back into prehistory and includes legends of fertility sprites, Merlin and Arthur, and Christian stories of crucifixion, resurrection, seraphim. The presence of St. Michael and all God's angels dominate the Christian imagination of the area and is reflected in place names and the names and decoration of many of its mysterious, magnetic pre-Norman churches. Not surprisingly it is a landscape that has inspired poets of the numinous: Henry Vaughn, Thomas Traherne, David Jones, Francis Horowitz, Anne Cluysenaar, Ruth Bidgood. In the company of these luminaries, I am the merest spark, but like them have heard voices in the land's streams and rivers, seen angels in the shadows moving up illuminated valleys, felt enfolding Presence in encircling mountains, been deeply moved by churches that witness to ancient, deeply rooted Christian tradition. To visit this area with a certain pre-Enlightenment openness can be to rediscover in its mists, shadows, and illuminated hours the holiness with which God has endowed all creation.[5]

5. More information on this area is found in A.G. Bradley, *In the March and Borderland of Wales* (1911; repr., Hereford: Lapridge Publishing, 1994); T. J. Hughes, *Wales's Best One Hundred Churches* (Bridgend: Seren Books, 2006); Peter J. Conradi, *At the Bright Hem of God: Radnorshire Pastoral* (Bridgend: Seren Books, 2009); John Leonard, *Churches of Herefordshire and Their Treasures* (Herefordshire: Logaston Press, 2000); John Tonkin, *Herefordshire* (London: B.T. Batsford, Ltd., 1977); and *Inventory of the Historical Monuments in Herefordshire* (London: Her Majesty's Stationery Office, 1931).

Along the Wye

On a glorious summer day
this border country rolls out
in a carpet of green turf,
the fertile result
of a blood-soaked history.
A place where armies marched,
kings were made and broken;
it was not peaceful
as it seems now.

Cistercians nestled their abbeys
among these verdant hills,
built their common life
around a prayer-soaked emptiness,
the cloister at their heart.
Now, though they point east
from darkness to light,
in their skeletal remains
only the wind chants the hours.

Border lands often murmur
of what was and might have been.
Like the Welsh it leads to,
this land sings.
God draws back the veil
to make a Golden Valley
between Black Mountains,
a place teeming with the life
of presence and past.

Skirrid

Benign beauty in verdant spring,
rosy crowned at sunset,
who would think
it marks a murder?

In a land of cwm and mountain
its great sky splitting
sets it apart from its sisters,
draws the eye upward
the mind to unfamiliar things:
terror of noonday dark,
death of light.

In this war weary world
where sword is never sheathed
and murder common as mud,
what would break a mountain?
What holds so high a holiness
that sorrow for its loss
would rend the good, green earth?

The Skirrid is a mountain with a great cleft that dominates the local landscape. The story is told that the mountain split at the moment of Christ's death.

"Cwm" is the Welsh word for a small valley.

The Cwm

Again, unearned blessing,
ever-new reprise,
spring in border country
redolent with blossom
where, in quintessential green,
stream's steady *basso*
accompanies bird's treble.

I press my senses against this place,
absorb serene energy
won through betrayal's pain,
bear it home in my cells,
talisman against terror,
shining place of retreat
in the soul's dark night.

"That They May Have Life"

Blackthorn in bloom and gorse,
in late afternoon
we threaded maze-like lanes
up to the hill farm
with the ancient trees,
with the magical view.

Nipping at heels,
a blue-eyed sheepdog
herds us to the door.
The old brother ushers us in
and disappears
before his sister offers tea.

A tiny lamb lies
on a sack by the hearth
working hard to breathe.
"We'll know by tonight
if he'll make it," she says.

"He" not "it," she says.
No anonymous thing,
but a dear, gendered one
gasps for precious life,
rib cage working like bellows.

The mystery of life and death
plays itself out
on a flagstone kitchen floor,
the womb center of a home
that welcomes strangers,
that nurtures life.

Sheep of His pasture,
lambs on His hearth,
we are fragile creatures
waiting in the gloaming
to be called by name,
hoping to rise from the dead.

St. Mary's Church, Craswall

We didn't intend to come here,
were on our way to Hay,
to bank, books, lunch.
But her presence there,
Queen of Monnow Valley,
required attendance.

She is an unprepossessing church,
low, square, sturdy,
weather-boarded bell turret
(perhaps without a bell?),
old fives court, a cockpit on the north,
the west end walled for a school.
Stone seating on the south faces
the base for a preaching cross
where only rotten wood remains.

The porch door was locked,
but the nave door—
a thing of old, solid planks,
iron bands, heavy, circular handle—
groaned into carefully tended space.
Lit by perpendicular east windows
from a priory Edward IV dissolved.

In dull morning light,
the few bits of brass gleamed;
the pots of local flowers were fresh;
the life of something ancient
that guidebooks never mention
was alive and well and palpable.

One never knows when errands
on ordinary, overcast days
will swing open into places of love.

The Church of St. Mary and St. David, Kilpeck

Remote, beautifully proportioned,
made of local red stone,
it stands as it did
in the twelfth century:
solid, rooted, prayerful.

Wondrously decorated with
a green man, a Sheela-na-gig,
creatures of a whimsical imagination
that wisely invited
the humorous and hideous to church.

Supported by snakes and vines,
a heavy Norman doorway
summons the pilgrim,
"rekindle hope
all ye who enter here."

Inside, the eye is drawn by arches
through nave to choir
to where, above the altar,
David plays his harp
in a small, colored window.

It is a church for poets
who let the lovely and the lewd,
the beastly and the beautiful,
the pagan and the pious
sit down together.

It is a church for dreamers
and those who know God
delights to dwell
in juxtapositions, silence
and stones that cry out.

It is a church for those
with eyes baptized
in the belly of a font
that stands with its feet
on the Rock of Ages.

Sheela-na-gig on Kilpeck Church

Squatting under the eaves,
lewdly grinning down at us,
exposing yourself to all comers,
who brought you to church?
What raucous imagination
dared make you
an ecclesiastical decoration?

One which loved fleshly life,
knew sex is hilarious
and procreation normal;
one which explored
a woman's body and found
treasures in darkness
and riches in secret places.

A Sheela-na-gig is a female figure exposing herself. One finds some form of this odd, crude figure in a remarkable number of ancient churches.

Green Man

I never met a Green Man
until I stumbled upon him
in Welsh border country.
Then I found him
in every church:
a leafy mask,
a grinning Pan
smirking fertility
in a dusty corner;
or a male head
looking slightly surprised
disgorging vegetation
down a pillar,
over a door frame;
or the hint of a face
furtive behind leaves,
Adam hiding among the trees.

Old as God's third day
and every bit as good,
you flourished
long before the church
grafted you in.
Now, though we try
to tame you, name you
in guidebooks

and art history,
you burst forth
make even stone live,
turn it to bread
that feeds my hunger
for irrepressible reality.
Root it deep within us,
this healing wholeness,
this wild profusion of life.

Abbey Dore, Ascensiontide

No longer lord of the lands
or a center of chant and commerce,
a shadow of your former self,
your crossing was salvaged
for a parish church.
The Cistercians were domesticated,
brought down to lay level,
mortified for mortals.

Suddenly, without warning,
singing an Ascension hymn
at an ordinary evensong,
your transfiguration
transforms us.
Lifted up by your coming down,
we need not gaze at heaven
having glimpsed it here.
Feet firmly on good earth,
our voice bears witness to joy

which is always in short supply,
which always enlivens what is dead.
Cloistered spirits
of long departed monks
rise up and attend our song.

Even the martial cries
of your malign neighbors
are stilled by the power of praise.
We sing in your nave.
You rise from your grave.

Norman Churches, Herefordshire

Escaping turbulent Oxford
I used to bike to Iffley,
sit in the shadows
of that Norman church
and breathe easier.
I did not know
what drew me,
only that it soothed,
calmed, centered.

Thirty years later
I glimpse the why
here, in these churches
built of local stone,
churches that seem
to rise from earth
without human help
as naturally as hedgerows
and as full of life.

Their square simplicity
is softened
by arch and apse.
No ornate fan vaulting
draws the eye upward.

Homey dog-toothed arches
tie walls firmly to floor,
make the place solid,
embracing, permanent.

Unpretentious churches
house a practical
life of spirit.
No lace cuffs ever offered
or incense accompanied
the coarse broken bread,
the pewter cup
of rough wine
that tastes of earth.

Unpretentious churches
root the life of this land
in the practice of prayer,
at many crossroads
quietly offer all comers
an invitation to pause,
to rest, to remember
that peace passes
understanding.

Wales

As any person of Welsh descent will cheerfully tell you, Wales is a very different kettle of fish from England or Ireland, or even Scotland with which, in some ways, it has the most affinity. Wales was never completely ruled by either the Briton or Norman kings. The description of St. David, patron of Wales, in the Episcopal Church's *Lesser Feasts and Fasts* summarizes well the situation:

> Despite the overwhelming victory of the pagan Angles, Saxons, and Jutes in the fifth century, one part of Britain continued in the ways of Christianity—Wales, the land west of the Wye River. In this last stronghold of the old Britons, the faith sprung from Glastonbury continued to flourish.[1]

Wales's remoteness and mountain terrain protected it, much as our towns and hamlets in the Appalachians have been protected. So did the fierceness with which its warriors defended their homeland (another characteristic we share!). The ancient Welsh were a fierce and fiercely religious group. Even the vigorous nineteenth-century attempts to "Anglicize" the Welsh, the

---

1. *The Proper for the Lesser Feasts and Fasts 2000* (New York: Church Publishing, Inc., 2001), 172.

harshness of that program in the schools, was not very successful. The language that system tried to stamp out is today heard from loudspeakers on train platforms and in the streets and shops all over Wales.

Welsh Christianity also developed its own way. Before the sixth century, the "age of the saints," there is little literary evidence. As in Scotland and Ireland, monasteries were founded, and, in time, those on the coasts were despoiled by the Norsemen. The Normans brought continental church influence to what of Wales they could conquer or reach. The austerity of the Cistercians was in consonance with local life and their lack of loyalty to the Normans must also have appealed, so their presence was strong in the country. The account of the 1188 journey through Wales of Baldwin, Archbishop of Canterbury, which was recorded by Gerald of Wales, makes engaging reading.[2] That nearly 90 percent of the output of Tudor and Stuart presses in Wales were religious books is, itself, telling. In the seventeenth century only a tiny percentage of the population was nonconformist: Baptist, Independent, Quaker, Presbyterian. After 1682 many Welsh Quakers and Baptists emigrated to Pennsylvania. Methodists remained in the Established Church until the Calvinistic Methodists (an indigenous Welsh denomination) left at the beginning of the nineteenth century, the period in which nonconformity grew to include about 75 percent of the populace at mid-century. The Anglican Church was disestablished in Wales by an Act in 1914

2. It is easily available in a modern edition. Gerald of Wales, *The Journey through Wales and The Description of Wales*, trans. Lewis Thorpe (London: Penguin Books, 1978).

that took effect in 1920.[3] Interestingly this seemed to have had the effect of strengthening Anglicanism.

The Anglican Church in Wales is no longer the "English Church," as witnessed to by its Welsh-English prayer book. Free Churches now include the Calvinistic Methodists, Baptists, and Independents, though the Wesleyan tradition is less strong. (They all came to West Virginia where I grew up!) In an address given when he was Archbishop of Wales, Glyn Simon spoke of the "special heritage in Wales of hundreds and hundreds of little ancient churches. . . . They are quite different from any in England. They are small and simple and very much home-made. They fit the landscape and the climate; they are the offerings of a poor people, harassed over the centuries by war and living on land very different from the rich and rolling counties of England."[4]

The landscape of Wales is similar to that of my own home, and when I read Richard Llewellyn's novel about the Welsh mining families, *How Green Was My Valley*, I already "knew" everyone in the book. The tradition of colliery bands and choirs of my youth were brought over by Welsh and Scots miners. In our Appalachian mountain hamlets, tiny, independent chapels dot the landscape where, as in Wales, an extraordinary musical tradition of hymn singing persists. Hymn-writer Ann Griffiths (1776–1805) is one of Wales's fine poets. In Wales no *eisteddfod*

3. A very good short summary of the history of the church in Wales is found in F. L. Cross and E. A. Livingstone, eds., *The Oxford Dictionary of the Christian Church* (New York: Oxford University Press, 1997).

4. Quoted in A. M. Allchin and Esther de Waal, eds., *Daily Readings from Prayers and Praises in the Celtic Tradition* (Springfield, IL: Templegate Publishers, 1986), 29. T. J. Hughes' sensitively written and beautifully illustrated book, *Wales's Best One Hundred Churches* (Bridgend: Seren, 2006) is an important addition to the literature on Welsh churches.

meets without singing competitions, recitations, and poetry competitions. (One of my treasured possessions is the small hand-embroidered purse I received for second prize in the hymn competition of the 2004 Longtown & District Eisteddfod.) Wizened is the heart and blind the eye that does not well up when it hears Bryn Terfel sing "Cwm Rhondda" ("Guide me, O thou great Jehovah").

Wales is, and always has been, a land of singers and poets. Many of Wales's modern and contemporary poets are poets of place.[5] One thinks immediately of Dylan Thomas and R. S. Thomas, of Ruth Bidgood and Anne Cluysenaar, and poems of the current Archbishop of Canterbury, Rowan Williams. The poetry division of the Welsh Books Council and Poetry Wales, Ltd. are two of the most active such organizations in Europe. The poems that follow are thematically in the tradition of Welsh Celtic spirituality, treating, as they do, religious sentiment, churches, landscape. They agree with the sentiments of T. Rowland Hughes's hymn "Tydi a Roddaist," "Oh! Save us from the dawning of a day / when our hearts are no longer driven to song."[6]

5. For an important recent study see Peter J. Conradi, *At the Bright Hem of God: Radnorshire Pastoral* (Bridgend: Seren, 2009).

6. Quoted from the liner notes of Bryn Terfel's CD *We'll Keep A Welcome*, Deutsche Grammophon (2000).

Hwyl

I do not know how to say
this vowel-free Welsh word
that means "fervor"
or perhaps "mood,"
"usually religious."
But I know its reality.
It catches me suddenly
as I turn a corner,
find a familiar place
utterly other, utterly new.
Or, when on my habitual walk,
the material of the trees
and lake and hills,
the world in all its color,
becomes a cut-out,
and I see through it
dark infinity behind it;
when the veil over reality
blows back as if on a breath,
and the world vibrates,
glows ever so slightly
with the white energy
of the source it manifests.
Ah, then—*hwyl.*

Dry Stone Walls, Wales

Land of moving light in open fields,
of dark, mysterious valleys,
like the saint's expansive holiness
unable to fit its inhabited space,
the beauty of Wales is so vast
it must be broken into manageable bits.

So the great, windswept mountains,
the green, rolling hills,
are marked off by walls,
flat plates of gray stone,
jigsaw of pieces fit lovingly together
by a practiced hand, an artist's eye.

Some, like those up Offa's Dyke, are sharp,
wear only the lichen of a century or so.
Others, in narrow, secret lanes
winding down from old Penallt church,
are immensely old, rounded green with moss
as if earth reaches up to claim her own.

But the sturdiest walls are unseen,
like the cherubim's flaming sword
protect the secret of the makers in stone,
their connection to the Keeper of wanderers,
the Keeper of all lost things,
the meticulous care of that keeping.

St. Melangell's Rabbits

At the edge of green field
beyond the protection
of tall grass, hedgerow,
the rabbit was grooming,
paws at work on face, ears,
brown body fur already sleek.
I drew much too close.
The wee beast never paused
in the work of washing,
having only pink slits
in place of ebony eye beads.
I looked on a long time
then clucked my tongue.
The rabbit drew down,
flattened its ears.
Our hearts beat fast,
our bodies bellows
wary with waiting,
both knowing ours a world
that crucifies weakness.

Watchful St. Melangell,
beckon and draw us all,
blind, vulnerable creatures
beneath the hem
of the healing garment.

The legend of St. Melangell tells the story of how the beautiful young noblewoman left Ireland for Wales to live a life of prayer. Once when Prince Brochwel was hunting on his land, he pursued a hare into a bramble thicket where he found Melangell praying—with the hare hiding in the folds of her clothes. He called off his dogs (which had refused to approach the saint) and gave her the surrounding lands for her sanctuary. "Her way of life was such that wild hares surrounded her as though they had been tame." So says the introduction of a beautiful collection of poems about St. Melangell edited by Anne Cluysenaar and Norman Schwenk, *The Hare That Hides Within* (Cardigan: Parthian, 2004), ix–x.

St. Issui's Church, Patricio

"I, too, something will make and joy in the making."

The Well

After days of deluge
streams roar down the mountain
so I heard the holiness
before I saw the place,
still green in November,
still with the sound of water,
filled with the verdancy of life.
How far back does primeval go?

To know this place,
to drink its healing water,
we are forced to our knees,
go down to the darkness,
to primeval waters older even
than the church's ancient font,
to the holiness before His coming
here which has always been.

+++

The Water

The constant companion
for most of the journey
was the howl of wind, dark sky,
rain blown horizontally
in peppery tattoo on windows.
Except for the bright,
timeless day
in the hidden valley,
on the holy hill,
place of living water.
Shining leaves of holly and ivy
encircled the ancient stone well
where we, like shepherds,
bent to adore.
Then took the path up
the mossy green birth canal
and into the light,
entered a church
on whose walls even death
breaks into dancing
and rabbit-eared dragons
nibble only vegetation.
Heavy with holiness,
but ever so gently,
it cracks internal resistance
so one wades without wariness
into Ezekiel's river,
deep enough to swim in,
impossible to cross.

The Shrine

Your image is modern
but the sculptor knew you,
your luminous solitude.
It fits your simple shrine
plain as the hills, the people,
the heart of this pilgrim
who finds comfort
in the solid north wall
no demons can breach,
the light that comes
from above and behind,
the riven stone revealing
the narrowest glimpse
of holiness far away,
the six consecration crosses.
(Five for His wounds;
one for our woundedness?)
I rest my head
on the stone altar
of your holiness,
like the one black sheep
in the churchyard,
know myself safely home.

This poem sequence is in thanksgiving for Stephanie and James Coutts whose Welsh hospitality has brought me great joy and happy familiarity with churches like St. Issui's and that at Old Penallt.

The epigraph for this sequence is a line from a tombstone at the church.

Our Lady of Old Penallt Church

She presides from a niche in the nave
crowned in medieval mode,
blue drapery distressed,
Her Child cradled close,
but Her gaze on us.

She was hacked from a holly bole.
As the old people tell it
holly grew under Christ's feet,
spiny leaves and red berries
His suffering and blood.

Pagan tree of masculine attributes,
talisman against evil sprites,
lord of the dark half of the year,
holly stood for Saturnalia, Lammas,
firstfruits, sacrificed gods.

Hard wood prized by smiths,
holly burns with searing flame,
like Her gaze, Her *fiat*, Her life.
Man-maid, archetypal mother,
the Holly bears the Crown.

St. Non's Well, St. David's

It erupted in a thunderstorm
as St. David came into the world.
Fitting, somehow, that the Waterman
be born between spring and sea,
born in a hut of purple stone
on the killing black cliffs
where the known world ends.

Our pilgrimage begins here
in slippery channels of living water.
Thrust from the thighs of a storm,
the fortunate are born on a day like this:
sharp wind, bright sun, green fields,
blackthorn in pristine bloom,
the royal gold of gorse.

Within sight and sound of the sea
we sign ourselves with her water,
know with quiet clarity
we are born for rebirth,
see with our own eyes
the dark horizon disappear
in brilliant light.

This poem is a thank-you gift for Leah Wright with whom I first visited St. David's and
St. Non's well, one of nine wells around St. David's that were part of its pilgrimage tradition
and the one associated with his mother, St. Non.

St. David's Cathedral

Prelates' palaces aren't our place,
but the house of God,
the bones of David, belong to us.
Nestled in an earthen bowl
as if God held it in cupped hands,
we come to it from above,
descend from our sufficiency
to his palace of prayer,
to our needs and knees.

To enter this purple cathedral
is to enter the solidity of stone,
a millennium of human yearning.
It is to be struck down, not
by elaborate roof, carved crucifix,
but by cavernous quietude,
cut by shafts of light
from mercifully colorless windows.

His old shrine is easy to miss,
but his box of bones is magnetic,
draws one like moth to flame
to private chapel behind public altar
where, under the eye of Gerald
who told some of its story,
one joins the viscous silence,
has world-weary wings singed,
dies to be reborn in praise.

Because of St. David's reputation, and his biography written by Rhgygfarch, bishop of St. David's from 1088 to 1096, his cathedral and monastic foundation became a pilgrimage destination. So important was St. David's in this respect that in the medieval period two pilgrimages to St. David's equaled one to Rome. As the town was on the main westward road to Ireland, many stopped to pray and, if they were of high standing, to visit at the magnificent Bishop's Palace, the remains of which are still very much in evidence.

"Gerald" is Gerald of Wales (Giraldus Cambrensis, ca. 1146–1223), archdeacon of Brecon and twice elected, but never consecrated as, bishop of St. David's. He wrote an engaging account of his travels through Wales (see note 2, p. 71) and a description of its topography.

Tymawr Convent, Wales

Not far from Tintern Abbey and near the town of Monmouth in Wales is the lovely Tymawr Convent of the Society of the Sacred Cross. The community is a outgrowth of the Oxford Movement having been founded in an Anglo-Catholic parish in Chichester in 1914. After World War I, it was reestablished in 1923 with the great assistance of Fr. G. Northcott, C.R. It was recognized in 1932 as an Anglican community. Today the core community is very small but keeps the monastic hours in an extraordinary chapel made from local stone. The community encourages and is supported by "Alongsiders," men and women who come to share the community's life for shorter or longer periods but are not vowed members. The sixty-five or so acres belonging to Tymawr is remarkable land, beautiful and full of its own energy.[1] My experience is that Tymawr Convent (and other communities that live close to their land) maintains in today's very different world the original monastic spirit of Celtic Christianity. It has been my privilege over the last ten years or so to spend significant time with this community. All of the following poems were inspired by and are gratefully dedicated to the sisters and Alongsiders at Tymawr. Several of the poems were

1. For more on the community and contact information visit their web site or write to Tymawr Convent, Lydart, Monmouth NP25 4RN, Wales.

published in the Dominican Order's Irish journal *Spirituality* and subsequently by the Tymawr community in a small chapbook, and I am grateful for permission to reprint those poems here.

Guest Room

In an earthenware jug on the desk
a twig of oak laden with acorns,
a branch of holly bending with berries.

In this house made holy
for Christ and His friends
two ancient symbols—
the tree of strength and endurance,
the tree of sacrifice and love—
are plunged in the same water,
given to make the stranger guest,
received with gratitude and delight,

        an image of peace
between the dark wisdom of the Old Ways,
and the golden Christ Who dances
off the gray stone walls
of his own guest-welcoming room.

The front wall of the chapel at Tymawr is dominated by a life-sized wooden crucifix that, in morning light, is indeed golden.

Poetic Justice: Berrying

My forearms look as if
I have been fighting cats.
When I bathe, the soap smarts.
But all I carry away from the day
I picked raspberries for Sr. Cara
is the delicious memory
of a warm autumn morning;
canes taller than I am
gently dancing around me;
the friendliness of an English robin;
gratitude for inclusion, a job to do;
and enormous groundedness.
I got the ripe, red raspberries.
It is poetic justice that
they also got me.

Megaliths, Tymawr

Plinth and pillar,
these rough columns,
three solid stone sisters,
hold up a sheep shed now.
But they are Other,
time travelers, visitors
from an ancient,
undomesticated age.

When I dared place my hand
flat on their rough-hewn sides,
I felt a faint, throbbing beat,
the energy of dances by firelight,
beseeching songs of the solstices,
primeval yearning
for a predictable God.

Great stones stand in a farm field
co-opted for ordinary duty.
But no one can co-opt the power
which resonates around them
recalling a time when we knew
the world is more than what appears,
that there are messages in everything
and messengers everywhere.

We are thin now, shiver in the wind.
Our souls are malnourished
as autumn shorn sheep
which can only wander aimlessly
eating grass in the presence of mystery,
afraid of the darkness
behind the stones.

This poem is for Tymawr's Mother Mary Jean (now of blessed memory) who told me about their megaliths and said they would be removed "over my dead body." There are on the convent's property at least four megaliths of immense age and mysterious, pulsating energy.

Chapel

In the absences between the Hours
I sit in the secret, narrow space
between solid stone altar and wall,
feel the pulsating frequency
of potent, ancient sanctity.

Is it the spring of water
architects could not staunch
that runs beneath the stones,
the fiery need of primitive prayers
once whispered in its maternal ear?

Is it that this local stone
drank the blood of Welsh miners
lured deep by black diamonds,
sustained by the mighty music
of their chapel's ghostly echoing here?

What gives this spare space
extraordinary, vibratory grace,
so terrible, healing, powerful
I must remove my shoes,
drink it in with the soul in my feet?

There are depths not ours to know,
mysteries beyond the mind.
I raise my eyes to the Son
of living wood, the golden Corpus,
hope that to receive is enough.

Requiem for a Small, Brown Bat

A soft, crumbled thing
lay at chapel entrance.
I thought it
the desiccated head
of a fallen rose.
But I picked up
a tiny, brown bat,
wings folded,
head bowed in death.

It had whizzed through Vespers.
I wondered whether
it found a home
under this timbered roof.

Poor, wee thing.
I carried it carefully
down the cloister,
put it to earth
by the kitchen door,
pondered how many
fragile things
have died in chapels,
grieved for them all.

Remembering Mystery

Palm Sunday dawned darkly
rain spattering the windows
in a wind more arctic than vernal.
Not a day for flowers and lace.
Life is not yet greatly in evidence,
no leafy branches to wave, walk on,
a paucity of glory, laud, honor.

All this long week we weave
great mufflers of words,
wind them around our throats,
a thin congregation
huddled in hard pews,
shivering innumerable psalms
into implacable space.

Are we to the martyred God
the annoying, obsessive sparrow
which, all last week, fluttered
at my library window
battering futilely for entrance
to the knowing place?

All this long, terrible week
we will multiply words,
forty-, sixty-, a hundred-fold,
mutter the ancient, holy ones
as if afraid heaven might hear,
forget Love's last meal command:
This do in remembrance.

Remembering mystery requires muteness
which stuns high priests, Pilates,
all incessant prattlers of ignorance.
Surely there is more resurrection
in the brave and listening primroses,
in the wind-whipped daffodils,
their trumpets bowed and silent.

This poems is for Br. John Mercer, their own "St. Jack of Tymawr."

Easter Confession

I sat for an afternoon
looking out on gnarled trees
of immense size and antiquity
not yet budded, but brooding
over great swaths of daffodils
floating on green March.
Nothing animate moved,
but the garden was inhabited,
peopled by shades of those
I loved imperfectly, badly even
if love be judged.
I long to have been wiser
than I could have been,
needed less, given more,
been truer to passion
and the Eastering soon upon us.
I wept bitter, penitential tears
blue as Forget-Me-Nots.

Orchard

An avenue of apple trees
marks the way to the burial place,
the place of resurrection,
reflects an ancient impulse,
like the cry of the owl's
nightly chant in this nocturnal nave.

Avalon, *abhlach*, the place of apples,
sacred and dangerous tree of Hesperides,
around their roots Cerridwen coils;
their hair hosts mistletoe beloved of Druids.
Every simple person knows
Eve tempted Adam with apples.

Apples bespeak plentitude
and love's consummation.
This year, orchard and grave
had bountiful harvests.
"Keep them as the apple of thine eye,"
we chant with our lips.

In our hearts we pray,
"leave but a single apple, Lord,
to ensure the future crop,"
while in places we cannot imagine
birds are planting wildings,
and the work of God goes on.

In memoriam: Sr. Laurie, SSC, who loved Tymawr's orchard, chose this poem to be read at
her funeral, and made me an "honorary Canadian."

Leaving Tymawr after Requiem Mass

In the center of chapel,
heart of the heart,
remembrance candles
burn down to sand
that holds and consumes them.

As the flames depart
wisps of smoke
circle dance upward,
mysteriously illumined
by the burning left behind.

May all our leaving
and remaining
always be like this:
a receiving and releasing
of the gifts of light.

Acknowledgments
and Thanksgivings

Excerpt from T. Rowland Hughes's hymn "Tydi a Roddaist," quoted from the liner notes of Bryn Terfel's CD *We'll Keep A Welcome*, Deutsche Grammophon (2000). Used by permission of Aureus Publishing Limited.

A briefer version of the "Tymawr" sequence originally appeared in *Spirituality* 13, no. 72 (2007). Used by permission. Thanks are due, as well, to the sisters of the Society of the Sacred Cross for their privately printed pamphlet of the sequence.

"St. Mary's Church, Craswell" originally appeared in *The Cantilupe Journal* 20 (Summer 2009). Used by permission of *The Cantilupe Journal*, The Cathedral Church of the Blessed Virgin Mary and St. Ethelbert, Hereford. My gratitude to Esther de Waal for taking me to this and so many other lovely churches.

"Brendan the Navigator" and "The Dove flew" from the St. Columba sequence originally appeared in *The Merton Journal* 8, no. 1 (2001). Used by permission.

An earlier and briefer version of the "Celtic Culdees" sequence of poems appeared in my small collection *The Heart's Lands*

(Abergavenny, Wales: Three Peaks Press, 2001). "Along the Wye," "The Church of St. Mary and St. David, Kilpeck," "Sheela-na-gig on Kilpeck Church," "Green Man," "Abbey Dore, Ascensiontide," and "Norman Churches, Herefordshire" also appeared in this volume. My profound gratitude to Michael Woodward, editor of Three Peaks Press, who saw merit in my work and published my first two collections of verse, and just when I was giving it all up.

Iona is a very important place for me. The worship led by the Iona Community in the abbey is sustaining. The staff at the St. Columba Hotel enhances with creature comforts my pilgrimages to the tiny island where it was my joy to meet James (of blessed memory) and Maggie Hughes, now Iona friends. And my thanks to Neil Paynter, editor at Wild Goose Publications, for ongoing encouragement and a good cuppa in Glasgow.

Without invitations from the Society of the Sacred Cross at Tymawr Convent to give retreats there I might never have come to know the Borders and Wales. Without the lavish hospitality of Esther de Waal and the Rev. James and Stevie Coutts (and wee Bertie) I would never have seen so much of the land they love, come to know it "from the inside," and love it as well. Sincerest and most heartfelt thanks to each.

And thank you for reading the book right through to the acknowledgments!

The following permissions were still in process at the time of publication:

"Hwyl" originally published in *Quattrocentro* 5 (2006).

"That They May Have Life" originally published in *Fire* 25 (March 2005).

Bibliography

Primary Sources

Adomnan of Iona. *Life of St. Columba*. Translated by Richard Sharpe. London: Penguin Books, 1995.

Carmichael, Alexander. *Carmina Gadelica*. Hudson, NY: Lindisfarne Press, 1992/94.

Davies, Oliver, ed. *Celtic Spirituality*. New York: Paulist Press, 1999.

Davies, Oliver, and Fiona Bowie, eds. *Celtic Christian Spirituality: An Anthology of Medieval and Modern Sources*. New York: Continuum, 1995.

Gerald of Wales. *The Journey through Wales/The Description of Wales*. Translated by Lewis Thorpe. London: Penguin Books, 1978.

Jackson, Kenneth Hurlstone, ed. *A Celtic Miscellany*. London: Penguin Books, 1951/71.

Secondary Sources

Backhouse, Janet. *The Lindisfarne Gospels: A Masterpiece of Book Painting*. London: The British Library, 1995.

Bradley, Ian. *Celtic Christianity*. New York: St. Martin's Press, 1999.

Chadwick, Nora K. *The Age of the Saints in the Early Celtic Church*. London: Oxford University Press, 1961.

de Blacam, Hugh. *The Saints of Ireland: The Life Stories of SS Brigid and Columcille*. Milwaukee: Bruce Publishing Co., 1942.

de Waal, Esther. *The Celtic Way of Prayer*. London: Hodder & Stoughton, 1996.

———. *Every Earthly Blessing: Recovering the Celtic Tradition*. Harrisburg, PA: Morehouse Publishing, 1999.

———. "A Fresh Look at the Synod of Whitby: A Mark of Unity and Reconciliation," in *I Have Called You Friends*. Barbara Braver, ed. Cambridge, MA: Cowley Publications, 2006.

———. *To Pause at the Threshold: Reflections on Living on the Border*. Harrisburg, PA: Morehouse Publishing, 2001.

Harding, Mike. *A Little Book of the Green Man*. London: Aurum Press, 1998.

Harte, Jeremy. *The Green Man*. Norwich, England: Pitkin Books/Jarrold Publishing, 2001/04.

Leatham, Diana. *The Story of St. David of Wales*. London: Garraway (Wales), Ltd., 1952.

Low, Mary. *Celtic Christianity and Nature: Early Irish and Hebridean Traditions*. Edinburgh: Edinburgh University Press, 1996.

MacKey, James P., ed. *An Introduction to Celtic Christianity*. Edinburgh: T & T Clark, 1989.

McNeill, John T. *The Celtic Churches: A History A.D. 200 to 1200*. Chicago: University of Chicago Press, 1974.

Meehan, Aidan. *The Celtic Design Book*. New York: Thames & Hudson, 2007.

Moorhouse, Geoffrey. *Sun Dancing*. New York: Harcourt Brace, 1997.

Newell, J. Philip. *Listening for the Heartbeat of God: A Celtic Spirituality*. New York: Paulist Press, 1997.

———. *One Foot in Eden: A Celtic View of the Stages of Life*. New York: Paulist Press, 1999.

O'Donohue, John. *Anam Cara: A Book of Celtic Wisdom*. New York: Harper Collins, 1997.

O'Loughlin, Thomas. *Journeys on the Edge: The Celtic Tradition*. Maryknoll, NY: Orbis Press, 2000.

O'Malley, Brendan. *St. David's*. Norwich, England: Canterbury Press, 1997.

Robertson, Jenny. *Strength of the Hills: Understanding Scottish Spirituality*. Oxford, England: Bible Reading Fellowship, 2001.

Sheldrake, Philip. *Living Between Worlds: Place and Journey in Celtic Spirituality*. Boston: Cowley Publications, 1996.

Ward, Benedicta. *High King of Heaven: Aspects of Early English Spirituality*. Kalamazoo, MI: Cistercian Publications, 1999.

———. *A True Easter: The Synod of Whitby 664 AD*. Oxford, England: SLG Press, 2007.

Westwood, J. D. *Celtic and Anglo-Saxon Art and Ornament*. Mineola, NY: Dover Publications, Inc., 2007.

Literary/Imaginative Works

Bidgood, Ruth. *Symbols of Plenty: Selected Poems*. Norwich, England: Canterbury Press, 2007.

Buechner, Frederick. *Brendan: A Novel*. San Francisco: Harper & Row, 1988.

———. *Godric: A Novel*. San Francisco: Harper & Row, 1980.

Cluysenaar, Anne, and Norman Schwenk, eds. *The Hare That Hides Within: Poems about St. Melangell*. Cardigan, Wales: Parthian, 2004.

Finlay, Alec, ed. *Carmichael's Book*. Edinburgh: Scotland: Morning Star Publications, 1997.

Heath, Jennifer. *On the Edge of Dream: The Women of Celtic Myth and Legend*. London Penguin/Plume, 1998.

Steven, Kenneth C. *Iona: Poems*. Edinburgh: St. Andrew Press, 2000/03.

Storhaug, Glenn, ed. *The Kilpeck Anthology*. Madley, Herefordshire: Five Seasons Press, 1981; reissued by Charlbury, Oxford: The Senecio Press, n.d.

Thurston, Bonnie. *The Heart's Lands*. Abergavenny, Wales: Three Peaks Press, 2001.

Waddell, Helen, trans. *Beasts and Saints*. London: Constable and Company, Ltd., 1934/53.

Prayers/Devotional Collections

Adam, David. *A Desert in the Ocean: The Spiritual Journey According to St. Brendan the Navigator*. New York: Paulist Press, 2000.

———. ed. *The Wisdom of the Celts*. Oxford, England: Lion Publishing, 1996. (David Adams has written several collections of Celtic-type prayers.)

Allchin, A. M., and Esther de Waal. *Daily Readings from Prayers & Praises in the Celtic Tradition*. London: Darton, Longman, Todd, 1986.

Millar, Peter W. *An Iona Prayer Book*. Norwich, England: Canterbury Press, 1998.

n.a., *The Iona Community Worship Book*. Glasgow: Wild Goose Publications, 1991/94. (Wild Goose Publications is the printing house of the Iona Community [www.iona.org.uk] and provides a wealth of material for exploration.)

Ward, Benedicta, ed. and trans. *Christ Within Me: Prayers and Meditations from the Anglo-Saxon Tradition*. Kalamazoo, MI: Cistercian Publications, 2008.